MY HOUSE

D095135H

Also by Nikki Giovanni

Black Feeling, Black Talk/Black Judgement
Re: Creation
Spin a Soft Black Song
Gemini

MY HOUSE

Poems by

Nikki Giovanni

QUILL

New York   1983

Copyright © 1972 by Nikki Giovanni

All rights reserved. No part of this book may be reproduced or utilized in any form or by any means, electronic or mechanical, including photocopying, recording, or by any information storage or retrieval system, without permission in writing from the Publisher. Inquiries should be addressed to Permissions Department, William Morrow and Company, Inc., 1350 Avenue of the Americas, New York, N.Y. 10019.

It is the policy of William Morrow and Company, Inc., and its imprints and affiliates, recognizing the importance of preserving what has been written, to print the books we publish on acid-free paper, and we exert our best efforts to that end.

Library of Congress Cataloging in Publication Data

Giovanni, Nikki.
  My house.

  I. Title.
PS3557.I55M9   1981   811'.54   81-2080
ISBN 0-688-05021 -2 (pbk.)   AACR2

Printed in the United States of America

        14   15

For Ellis
who is a cornerstone in My House

Foreword by Ida Lewis

It is said that when the subject is complicated try drawing a simple picture, but even to this writer, who is both friend and sometimes editor to poet Nikki Giovanni, she cannot be simply understood or explained—she must be experienced and felt. The judgement, however, has been offered before: Nikki Giovanni is the Princess of Black Poetry.

Wilberforce University, Black America's oldest institution of higher learning, conferred upon Nikki an Honorary Doctorate of Humanities in April of this year. When Nikki got their letter she called a group of her friends and invited us to dinner. We weren't told why, just to come. Her face beaming like Tommy's when he took his first step, she solemnly read the letter to us. "Isn't that wonderful?" she exclaimed. Unfortunately she had accepted a speaking engagement in a small Pennsylvania town for the night before the ceremony. Getting to Wilberforce on time would be a tricky problem. "I'll be there. We'll make them both," she resolved. She organized her family, sent her son to Wilberforce with his baby-sitter a day earlier, sent all of us out there, and was on the road herself all night long. Nikki arrived at Wilberforce tired and happy, falling into the line already marching into the hall without her cap or gown. "Did you think I wasn't coming?" she asked a senior in the Honor Guard teasingly. "No," was the girl's quiet reply, "we knew you'd be here on time."

She is adored not only because she is Black America's most celebrated word magician, but also because she is an extraordinary example of the young Black spirit enjoying a newly reopened life. "See what my motherfuckers got me," she said laughingly to the overflow crowd at Wilberforce. Her father looked shocked, but the seniors gave her four standing ovations. "You must do what you think is important the way you think it's important, being trapped neither by the past of your people nor your future personal hopes."

It is indeed among the marvels of Nikki's art that her work has so deeply penetrated the hearts of so many. But why is that so? Is it something shocking about her poetry, something lascivious? Is it those "Revolutionary Dreams" that delight and excite the iron palate of today's readers? I've seen Nikki mobbed in Bloomingdale's department store by Black and white customers; I've walked with her down Fifth Avenue and watched a man who was saying "hi" to her walk into an oncoming taxi. She rides her bicycle to Harlem to buy books at Micheaux's and draws a crowd. She was recently the first poet to do poetry on the Tonight show with Flip Wilson. But none of this has stopped her from answering her mail: from youngsters in private schools in Vermont, "Miss Giovanni, I love you. I go to private school—am I irrelevant?"; from men in prison who advise her on how her son should be reared. "Don't forget," she writes, "Angela Davis went to private school and Malcolm X graduated from prison." Her pragmatic existential idealism forces her to take each case, each person personally.

Nikki Giovanni is a product of the thunderous and explosive sixties, endowed with a powerful and inquiring mind absorbed with the Black America of that decade—our vision of ourselves. And, like a painter's brush, her life depicts what Black America can see and feel. "Service is the key," she says over and over again. "If I can't find a way to serve and be serviced we won't make it." This summer Nikki did a five-city free concert tour from Atlanta to Detroit. She feels each artist must present herself to the community that made her—must take that chance, since any artist in free concert is vulnerable, on rejection so that roots won't be upended. She organized the tour herself, asking for plane fare in some cases and in others not even that to reach people. "I'm not afraid of rejection," she states, "because if the people aren't with you you may as well get back." Her special love of churches and the South makes her want to tour the South as soon as she's able. "Don't you think it's strange," I asked her after she passed out at a college reading, "that you could write 'Poem for Aretha,' then turn around and do the same thing?" "But, Ida," she said very definitely, "I understand why *she* does it—why she keeps the pace up." Knowing I was going to lose, I asked why. "Because here you have some people who've never gotten what they asked for—nothing—and they ask for you, that you would make them feel better or help them understand, plus they give a lot to you, you know? I guess love is the word. Because you love them you try and you hope they try."

Give me one line, you might ask, that explains Nikki Giovanni: She has absorbed her atmosphere—she knows her world from chief to thief. In "Nikki-Rosa" she wrote five words that stated to the world a new commitment, "Black love is Black wealth," and made one quixotic judgement: ". . . they'll probably talk about my hard childhood and never understand that all the while I was quite happy." The world of Nikki Giovanni is very real, sometimes too real for comfort, too naked for delight. A person who enters that cavern of poetic adventures can never be the same again. But she asks no more of her readers than of herself. In *Gemini* she raked her emotions bare to write of the death of her grandmother—moved from her home of eighteen years for a cutoff of a cutoff, knowing that neither she nor her mother would ever be able to read that essay without crying, without wondering if more could have been done. "But it's important for Tommy to know."

One key to an understanding of Nikki is to realize the pattern of her conviction. The central core is always associated with her family: the family that produced her and the family she is producing. To Nikki family is love: love is family. She has reached a simple philosophy more or less to the effect that a good family spirit is what produces healthy communities, which is what should produce a strong (Black) nation. Ask Nikki Giovanni what she believes in most, and undoubtedly her reply would be, "My family, myself, and Tommy." "I think the sexual revolution," she ventured to me in a moment of frustration, "is going to be crucial. Why shouldn't a man learn to take care of children? Do you see all our men standing on a corner thinking they are warriors when the real war is over at the playground? Those guys have got to relate to Black kids. And understand that we understand that they are men." Tommy was walking down the hall to the elevator one morning. He stopped halfway and said, "Carry me." Nikki changed her ever present briefcase to her other arm and picked him up. "If you aren't a good father," she said, "I'll brain you." He put his thumb in his mouth. She never,

I noticed, said good husband, or good provider, but broke it to a basic. She doesn't believe you can worry about how things look—she only cares how things are and how things must or should become.

A most interesting aspect of her work is the poet's belief in individualism at a time when the trend in the Black community is away from the individual and toward the mass. She has been reproached for her individualist attitudes by her critics, who have attempted to use this attribute to stamp her as irrelevant. But Nikki Giovanni's greatness is not derived from following leaders, nor has she ever accepted the burden of carrying the revolution. Her struggle is a personal search for individual values in the Black community, whose values are what the young Black critic Edward Black has defined as "pre-individualist."

> In the pre-individualistic thinking of the Negro, the stress is on the group. Instead of seeing in terms of the individual the Negro sees in terms of "races," masses of people separated from other masses according to color. Hence, an act rarely bears intent against him as a Negro individual. He is singled out not as a person but as a specimen of an ostracized group. He knows that he never exists in his own right but only to the extent that others hope to make the race suffer vicariously through him.

Nikki Giovanni's views of the Black predicament take as significant its fundamental questions: Who am I? What am I? How did I come to be? How related are love of self (love of family, love of community, love of humanity) and revolution? She does not attempt to answer unanswerable questions; but in true Giovannian fashion she gives consent to independence, advises self-determination. She jealously guards her right to be judged as an individual, insisting that her "I" experiences from infancy to adulthood are unique to Nikki Giovanni—which may or may not be of special value to the community. She is as realistic as she is sentimental, understanding changes are won by both individual practicality and functional unity. "I write what I see," she says, "and I take responsibility for it. Why should thirty million people have to have me as a spokesman?" She believes in space and time—which her critics say we do not have—for people to see what she sees. "I love 'Ego Tripping' 'cause it's a happy poem, but if it's not useful I want my readers to feel free to reject that and choose something else. You know, I don't believe that just because you like movies you have to sit through a bad show. Nixon and them say that—'take us or reject the American way.' I think I can believe in the necessity for theater, but I can still pick what I want to see."

Nikki knows the necessity of remembering, for to remember is to be born again; to forget is to dwell in eternal darkness. She teaches us not only that the people of the past are very much alive, but that we must not judge them from our modern pinnacle of knowledge and awareness. Our ancestors had the attitudes of their time, and Nikki takes them as they were, as they were obliged to be. "Nobody," she says, "ever wakes up in the morning and says how can I hurt Black people today? Not even white people. People wake up and ask how can I get a little further ahead? We are the only people who will read someone out of the race—the entire nation—because we don't agree with them. That's really crazy when, if we just can assume that others have the integrity we say we possess, we would be that much stronger."

And she vows to go on peering into the shadows of the

past. Taking the most anguished of themes and personal experiences, she explores their manifold depths. She holds nothing back, examining areas of suffering and guilt, religious ecstasy and doubt, and the intriguing notion of transference of personality. Nikki Giovanni makes the dry old bones of her Black history live and march, clothing them in real flesh of armors of steel, in velvet, silk, and white gloves—raising the question of Black manhood, reviving the blues, and reminding us again and again of the wealth of Black love.

Reading Nikki Giovanni is an intoxicating experience. It is certainly by no means an act of escape. Her work excites all of one's nerves. The head spins, the soul is forever invaded; one is tempted to cry out, Amen! Nikki knows, as Marvin Gaye says, "People, we've got to believe in each other's dreams." For she writes about the central themes of our times, in which thirty million Blacks search for self-identification and self-love. Through the works of Nikki Giovanni one realizes that though the fire is just beginning to burn, the flame is three hundred years old. Nikki has taken this flame and built *My House*.

It is to our credit that while this young poet walks among us we recognize and celebrate her genius. Let the vibrant drums acclaiming her uncompromising poetic talents continue to fill the air with right on, princess, write on.

Contents

xviii

MY HOUSE

THE ROOMS INSIDE

Legacies

her grandmother called her from the playground
    "yes, ma'am"
    "i want chu to learn how to make rolls" said the old
woman proudly
but the little girl didn't want
to learn how because she knew
even if she couldn't say it that
that would mean when the old one died she would be less
dependent on her spirit so
she said
    "i don't want to know how to make no rolls"
with her lips poked out
and the old woman wiped her hands on
her apron saying "lord
    these children"
and neither of them ever
said what they meant
and i guess nobody ever does

    [27 jan 72]

Mothers

the last time i was home
to see my mother we kissed
exchanged pleasantries
and unpleasantries pulled a warm
comforting silence around
us and read separate books

i remember the first time
i consciously saw her
we were living in a three room
apartment on burns avenue

mommy always sat in the dark
i don't know how i knew that but she did

that night i stumbled into the kitchen
maybe because i've always been
a night person or perhaps because i had wet
the bed
she was sitting on a chair
the room was bathed in moonlight diffused through
those thousands of panes landlords who rented
to people with children were prone to put in windows

she may have been smoking but maybe not
her hair was three-quarters her height
which made me a strong believer in the samson myth
and very black

i'm sure i just hung there by the door
i remember thinking: what a beautiful lady

she was very deliberately waiting
perhaps for my father to come home
from his night job or maybe for a dream
that had promised to come by
"come here" she said "i'll teach you
a poem: *i see the moon*
            the moon sees me
            god bless the moon
            and god bless me"
i taught it to my son
who recited it for her
just to say we must learn
to bear the pleasures
as we have borne the pains

[10 mar 72]

A Poem for Carol

(May She Always Wear Red Ribbons)

when i was very little
though it's still true today
there were no sidewalks in lincoln heights
and the home we had on jackson street
was right next to a bus stop and a sewer
which didn't really ever become offensive
but one day from the sewer a little kitten
with one eye gone
came crawling out
though she never really came into our yard but just
sort of hung by to watch the folk
my sister who was always softhearted but able
to act effectively started taking milk
out to her while our father would only say
don't bring *him* home and everyday
after school i would rush home to see if she was still
there and if gary had fed her but i could never
bring myself to go near her
she was so loving
and so hurt and so singularly beautiful and i knew
i had nothing to give that would
replace her one gone eye

and if i had named her which i didn't i'm sure
i would have called her carol

[20 dec 71]

8

A Fishy Poem

i have nine guppies
there were ten but the mother died shortly
after the birth
the father runs up and down the aquarium
looking

at first i thought i wasn't feeding
them enough
so i increased and increased
until the aquarium was very very dirty
then i realized he was just a guppie
whose father was a goldfish
and he was only following
his nature

[11 jan 72]

Winter Poem

once a snowflake fell
on my brow and i loved
it so much and i kissed
it and it was happy and called its cousins
and brothers and a web
of snow engulfed me then
i reached to love them all
and i squeezed them and they became
a spring rain and i stood perfectly
still and was a flower

[3 feb 72]

Conversation

"yeah" she said "my man's gone too
been dead longer than you is old"
"what do you do" i asked
"sit here on the porch and talk to the old folk
i rock and talk and go to church most times"
"but aren't you lonely sometimes" i asked
"now you gotta answer yo own question"
"i guess the children help a lot   you got grandchildren
haven't you"
"oh the children they come and go always in a hurry
got something to do ain't no time for old folks
like me"
she squinted at the sun packing her jaw
with *bruton* snuff
"the old days done gone . . . and i say good-bye
peoples be going to the moon and all . . . ain't that
wonderful . . . to the moon"
and i said "i see stars all the time aretha franklin
and sly were at madison square garden recently"
"what you doing here" she asked
"i'm a poet" i said
"that ain't no reason to be uppity"
and the sun beat down on my head while
a dragonfly admonished my flippancy

but a blue and yellow butterfly sat on my knee
i looked her square in the eye
"i ain't gonna tell you" she said and turned her head
"ain't gonna tell me what" i asked
"what you asking me you gotta live to be seventy-nine
fore you could understand anyhow"
"now you being uppity" i said
"yeah but i earned it" she replied and shifting her wad
she clapped her hands and smiled
"you been here before"
and i said "yes ma'am but would you tell me just one thing
what did i learn"
and she spat out her juice
"honey if you don't know how can i"
i wanted to argue but the sun was too hot and the sky
too lazy and god heaved a sigh that swept under my blouse
and i felt me feeling a feeling
she crossed her legs at the ankle
and straightened her back
"tell you this" she said
"keep yo dress up and yo pants down and you'll be all
        right"
and i said impatiently "old lady you got it all wrong"
"honey, ain't never been wrong yet
you better get back to the city cause you one of them
technical niggers and you'll have problems here"

[8 dec 71]

12

Rituals

i always wanted to be a bridesmaid
honest to god
i could just see me floating
down that holy aisle leading
some dear friend to heaven
in pink and purple organza with lots and lots
of crinoline pushing the violets out from my dress
hem
or maybe in a more sophisticated endeavor
one of those lovely sky blue slinky numbers
fitting tight around my abounding twenty-eights
holding a single red rose white gloves open in the back
always forever made of nylon and my feet nestled gently
in *chandlers* number 699 which was also the price plus
one dollar to match it pretty near the dress color

wedding rituals have always intrigued me
and i'd swear to friends i wouldn't say goddamn not even
once no matter what neither would i give a power
sign but would even comb my hair severely
back and put that blue shit under my eyes
i swear i wanted to be in a wedding

[20 dec 71]

13

Poem for Stacia

i see wonder
in little things
like thorn figurines rowing
across my table
or stacia caring
by imposing which being
such a little thing wasn't
a big imposition
and i saw a rainbow
after a very cloudy day
but i looked down to swat
a mosquito and lost
it in the midst

[16 july 71]

The World Is Not
a Pleasant Place to Be

the world is not a pleasant place
to be without
someone to hold and be held by

a river would stop
its flow if only
a stream were there
to receive it

an ocean would never laugh
if clouds weren't there
to kiss her tears

the world is not
a pleasant place to be without
someone

[17 feb 72]

The Only Song I'm Singing

they tell me that i'm beautiful i know
i'm Black and proud
the people ask for autographs
i sometimes draw a crowd
i've written lots of poetry and other
kinds of books
i've heard that white men crumble
from one of my mean looks
i study hard and know my facts
in fact the truth is true
the only song i'm singing now is my song
of you

> *and i'm asking you baby please*
> *please somehow show me what i need*
> *to know so i can love you right*
> *now*

i've had great opportunities to move
the world around
whenever they need love and truth they call
me to their town
the president he called me up and asked
me to come down

but if you think you want me home i think
i'll stick around
   and i'm asking you baby please baby baby show me
   right now most of the things i need to know
   so i can love you somehow

   [8 jan 72]

The Butterfly

those things
which you so laughingly call
hands are in fact two
brown butterflies fluttering
across the pleasure
they give
my body

[21 feb 71]

I Remember

i remember learning you jump
in your sleep and smile
when you wake up

at first you cuddle
then one arm across my stomach
then one leg touching my leg then
you turn your back

but you smile when you wake up

i was surprised to know you don't care
if your amp burns all night and that you could
play *ohmeohmy* over and over again just
because you remembered

i discovered you don't like hair
in your bathroom sink and never step
your wet feet onto a clean rug

you will answer your phone
but you don't talk too long and you do
rub my toes and make faces
while you talk
and your voice told her anyway
that i was there

19

you can get up at three and make sandwiches
and orange juice and tell jokes
you sometimes make incoherent sentences
you snore
and you smile when you wake up

i know you cry when you're hurt
and curse when you're angry
and try when you don't feel
like it and smile at me
when you wake up

these things i learned through
a simple single touch
when fleshes clashed

[21 jan 72]

A Certain Peace

it was very pleasant
not having you around
this afternoon

not that i don't love you
and want you and need you
and love loving and wanting and needing you

but there was a certain peace
when you walked out the door
and i knew you would do something
you wanted to do
and i could run
a tub full of water
and not worry about answering the phone
for your call
and soak in bubbles
and not worry whether you would want something
special for dinner
and rub lotion all over me
for as long as i wanted
and not worry if you had a good idea
or wanted to use the bathroom

and there was a certain excitement
when after midnight you came home
and we had coffee
and i had a day of mine
that made me as happy
as yours did you

[9 jan 72]

When I Nap

when i nap
usually after 1:30
because the sun comes
in my room then
hitting the northeast
corner

i lay at the foot
of my bed and smell
the sweat of your feet
in my covers
while i dream

[27 apr 72]

Mixed Media

on my bedroom wall hang a poster
two pen and inks one oil one framed photograph
something with a lot of color that i don't
quite know its substance
and you
cause i got tired of bathing and oiling
and waiting for you to be too tired or
too drunk and when i realized it was your smile
that turned me on i engraved it
just above the shelf where the ash tray sits
i cut your eyes and ears and nose away
leaving your lips to open me
to a very energetic
sober brother

[1 feb 71]

24

Just a New York Poem

i wanted to take
your hand and run with you
together toward
ourselves down the street to your street
i wanted to laugh aloud
and skip the notes past
the marquee advertising "women
in love" past the record
shop with "The Spirit
In The Dark" past the smoke shop
past the park and no
parking today signs
past the people watching me in
my blue velvet and i don't remember
what you wore but only that i didn't want
anything to be wearing you
i wanted to give
myself to the cyclone that is
your arms
and let you in the eye of my hurricane and know
the calm before

and some fall evening
after the cocktails
and the very expensive and very bad

steak served with day-old baked potatoes
after the second cup of coffee taken
while listening to the rejected
violin player
maybe some fall evening
when the taxis have passed you by
and that light sort of rain
that occasionally falls
in new york begins
you'll take a thought
and laugh aloud
the notes carrying all the way over
to me and we'll run again
together
toward each other
yes?

[31 oct 70]

[Untitled]

there is a hunger
    often associated with pain
    that you feel
    when you look at someone
    you used to love and enjoyed
    loving and want
    to love again
    though you know you can't
that gnaws at you
    as steadily as a mosquito
    some michigan summer
    churning his wings
    through your window screen
because the real world
    made up of baby

clothes	*to be washed*
food	*to be cooked*
lullabies	*to be sung*
smiles	*to be glowed*
hair	*to be plaited*
ribbons	*to be bowed*
coffee	*to be drunk*
books	*to be read*
tears	*to be cried*
loneliness	*to be borne*

says you are a strong woman
    and anyway he never thought you'd really miss him

[4 june 72]

27

The Wonder Woman

(A New Dream—for Stevie Wonder)

dreams have a way
of tossing and turning themselves
around and the times
make requirements that we dream
real dreams for example
i wanted to be
a sweet inspiration in my dreams
of my people but the times
require that i give
myself willingly and become
a wonder woman

[29 sep 71]

Categories

sometimes you hear a question like "what is
your responsibility as an unwed mother"
and some other times you stand sweating profusely before
going on stage and somebody says "but you are used
        to it"
or maybe you look into a face you've never seen
or never noticed and you know
the ugly awful loneliness of being
locked into a mind and body that belong
to a *name* or *non-name*—not that it matters
cause *you* feel and *it* felt but you have
a planetrainbussubway—it doesn't matter—something
to catch to take your arms away from someone
you might have thought about
putting them around if you didn't
have all that shit to take you safely away

and sometimes on rainy nights you see
an old white woman who maybe you'd really care about
except that you're a young Black woman
whose job it is to kill maim or seriously
make her question
the validity of her existence
and you look at her kind of funny colored eyes
and you think

29

if she weren't such an aggressive bitch she would see
that if you weren't such a Black one
there would be a relationship but anyway—it doesn't matter
much—except you started out to kill her and now find
you just don't give a damn cause it's all somewhat
          of a bore
so you speak of your mother or sister or very good friend
and really you speak of your feelings which are too
          personal
for anyone else
to take a chance on feeling
and you eat that godawful food and you get somehow
through it and if this seems
like somewhat of a tentative poem it's probably
because i just realized that
i'm bored with categories

          [4 jan 72]

Straight Talk

i'm giving up
on language
my next book will be blank
pages of various textures and hues
i have touched in
certain spots and patterns
and depending upon the mood the reader can come
with me or take me somewhere else

    i smell blood a'cookin

"but why" i asked when she said "i'm afraid
to see men cry"
"because i depend" she replied "on their strength"
"but are they any less strong for crying
nylon stockings wear better if they're washed first"

    mommy said it's only pot
    luck but you can have some

science teaches us matter
is neither created nor destroyed
and as illogical as it is there is nothing
worthwhile but people
and lord knows how irrational we are

31

i'll just have a scrambled egg
if it's all right

the question turns on a spelling problem
i mean i hate
to squash a roach and thought about giving up
meat between the shadow
and the act falls the essence   encore!
the preceding paragraph was brought to you by the letter E
in the name of huemanity

an acorn to an ant
is the same as a white man to a Black JOB
enjoyed waiting on
the lord tell me
why can't i

and i'm glad i'm smart cause i know
smart isn't enough and i'm glad
i'm young cause "youth and truth are making love" i'm glad
i'm Black not only
because it's beautiful but because it's me
and i can be dumb and old and petty and ugly
and jealous but i still need love

your lunch today was brought to you
by the polytech branch of your local
spear o agnew association
HEY! this is straight talk!

have a good day

[7 jan 72]

32

Scrapbooks

it's funny that smells and sounds return
so all alone uncalled unneeded
on a sweaty night as i sit armed
with coffee and cigarettes waiting

sometimes it seems
my life is a scrapbook

i usta get 1.50 per week
for various duties unperformed
while i read *green dolphin street*
and *the sun is my undoing*
never understanding my exclusion
but knowing quite clearly the hero
is always misunderstood
though always right in the end

roy gave me a yellow carnation
that year for the junior prom

the red rose was from michael
who was the prettiest boy i'd ever known
he took me to the *jack and jill* dance
and left me sitting in the corner until
the slow drags came on then he danced
real tight and sweated out my bangs

i had a white leather monstrosity that passed
for taste in my adolescence pressed with dances
undanced though the songs were melodious

and somehow three or four books were filled
with proms and parties and programs that
my grandmother made me go to
for "culture" so that i could be
a lady
my favorite is the fisk book with clippings
of the *forum* and notes from the dean of women
saying "you are on social probation" and "you are
suspended from fisk"
and letters from my mother saying "behave yourself"
and letters from my grandmother reminding me
"your grandfather graduated fisk in 1905" and not
to try to run the school
but mostly notes from alvin asking when
was i coming over
again
i purchased a blue canvas notebook for the refrain

it's really something when you sit
watching dawn peep over apartment buildings
that seemed so ominous during the night and see
pages of smiling pictures   groups of girls throwing
pillows   couples staring nervously ahead as if they
think the kodak will eat them   someone with a ponytail
and a miles davis record   a lady with an afro pointing
joyously to a diploma   a girl in a brown tan and red
bathing suit holding a baby that looks like you

and now there is a black leather book filled
efficiently by a clipping service
and a pile of unanswered letters that remind
you to love those who love you
and i sit at dawn
all my defenses gone sometimes
listening to *something cool* sometimes
hearing *tears on my pillow*
and know there must be other books
filled with failures and family and friends
that perhaps one day i can unfold
for my grandchildren

[11 dec 71]

When I Die

when i die i hope no one who ever hurt me cries
and if they cry i hope their eyes fall out
and a million maggots that had made up their brains
crawl from the empty holes and devour the flesh
that covered the evil that passed itself off as a person
that i probably tried
to love

when i die i hope every worker in the national security
      council
the interpol the fbicia foundation for the development
      of black women gets
an extra bonus and maybe takes one day off
and maybe even asks why they didn't work as hard for us
      as they did
them
but it always seems to be that way

please don't let them read "nikki-roasa" maybe just let
some black woman who called herself my friend go around
      and collect
each and every book and let some black man who said it was
negative of me to want him to be a man collect every picture
and poster and let them burn—throw acid on them—shit
      on them as

they did me while i tried
to live

and as soon as i die i hope everyone who loved me learns
    the meaning
of my death which is a simple lesson
don't do what you do very well very well and enjoy it it
    scares white folk
and makes black ones truly mad

but i do hope someone tells my son
his mother liked little old ladies with
their blue dresses and hats and gloves that sitting
    by the window
to watch the dawn come up is valid that smiling at an old
    man
and petting a dog don't detract from manhood
do
somebody please
tell him i knew all along that what would be
is what will be but i wanted to be a new person
and my rebirth was stifled not by the master
but the slave

and if ever i touched a life i hope that life knows
that i know that touching was and still is and will always
    be the true
revolution

[9 jan 72]

[Untitled]

(For Margaret Danner)

one ounce of truth benefits
like ripples on a pond
one ounce of truth benefits like a ripple
on a pond
one ounce of truth
benefits like ripples on
a pond
as things change remember my smile

the old man said my time is getting near
the old man said my time
is getting near
he looked at his dusty cracked boots to say
sister my time is getting near
and when i'm gone remember i smiled
when i'm gone remember
i smiled
i'm glad my time is getting there

the baby cried wanting some milk
the baby cried needing some milk
the baby he cried for wanting
his mother kissed him gently

when i came they sang a song
when i was born they sang a song
when i was saved they sang a song
remember i smiled when i'm gone
remember i smiled when i'm gone
sing a good song when i'm gone
we ain't got long to stay

[28 feb 72]

THE ROOMS OUTSIDE

THE SECOND

My Tower

(For Barb and Anthony)

i have built my tower on the wings of a spider
spinning slippery daydreams of paperdoll fantasies
i built my tower on the beak of a dove
pecking peace to a needing woman

i have built my dreams on the love of a man
holding a nation in his palm asking me the time of day

i built my castle by the shore thinking
i was an oyster clammed shut forever
when this tiny grain i hardly noticed
crept inside and i spit around
and spit around and spun a universe inside
with a black pearl of immeasurable worth
that only i could spin around

i have borne a nation on my heart
and my strength shall not be my undoing
cause this castle didn't crumble
and losing my pearl made me gain
and the dove flew with the olive branch by harriet's route
to my breast and nestled close and said "you are mine"
and i was full and complete while emptying my wombs
and the sea ebbed ohhhhhhhhh
what a pretty little baby

[25 jan 71]

45

Poem

(*For Nina*)

we are all imprisoned *in the castle of our skins*
and some of us have said so be it
if i am in jail my castle shall become
my rendezvous
my courtyard will bloom with hyacinths and jack-in-the-
    pulpits
my moat will not restrict me but will be filled
with dolphins sitting on lily pads and sea horses ridden by
    starfish
goldfish will make love
to Black mollies and color my world Black Gold
the vines entwining my windows will grow butterflies
and yellow jackets will buzz me to sleep
the dwarfs imprisoned will not become my clowns
for me to scorn but my dolls for me to praise and fuss
with and give tea parties to
my gnomes will spin cloth of spider web silkness
my wounded chocolate soldiers will sit in evening coolness
or stand gloriously at attention during that midnight sun
for i would have no need of day patrol
if i am imprisoned in my skin let it be a dark world
with a deep bass walking a witch doctor to me for spiritual
consultation
let my world be defined by my skin and the skin of my
    people
for we   spirit to spirit   will embrace
this world

[12 jan 72]

46

Africa I

on the bite of a kola nut
i was so high the clouds blanketing
    africa
in the mid morning flight were pushed
away in an angry flicker
of the sun's tongue

a young lioness sat smoking a pipe
while her cubs waved up at the plane
look ida i called a lion waving
but she said there are no lions
in this part of africa
it's my dream dammit i mumbled

but my grandmother stood up
from her rocker just then
and said you call it
like you see it
john brown and i are with you
and i sat back for my morning
coffee

we landed in accra and the people
clapped and i almost cried wake up
we're home

and something in me said shout
and something else said quietly
your mother may be glad to see you
but she may also remember why
you went away

[11 july 71]

Africa II

africa is a young man bathing
in the back of a prison fortress

the guide said "are you afro-american
cape coast castle holds a lot for your people"

and the 18th century clock keeps perfect
time for the time it has

i watched his black skin turn foaming
white and wanted to see this magnificent
man stand naked and clean before me
but they called me to the dungeons where above
the christian church an african stood listening
for sounds of revolt

the lock the guide stated indicated a major once ran
the fort and the british he said had recently demanded
the lock's return
and i wanted the lock maybe for a door
stop to unstop the 18th century clock

"and there is one African buried
here   we are proud of him" he said
and i screamed NO there are thousands
but my voice was lost in the room

of the women with the secret passageway
leading to the governor's quarters

so roberta flack recorded a song
and les mccann cried but
a young african man on the rock
outside the prison where my people were
born bathed in the sunlight

and africa is a baby to be
tossed about and disciplined and loved
and neglected and bitten on its bottom
as i wanted to
sink my teeth into his thigh
and tell him he would never be
clean until he can
possess me

[11 july 71]

They Clapped

they clapped when we landed
thinking africa was just an extension
of the black world
they smiled as we taxied home to be met
black to black face not understanding africans lack
color prejudice
they rushed to declare
cigarettes, money, allegiance to the mother land
not knowing despite having read fanon and davenport
hearing all of j.h. clarke's lectures, supporting
nkrumah in ghana and nigeria in the war that there was once
a tribe called afro-americans that populated the whole
of africa
they stopped running when they learned the packages
on the women's heads were heavy and that babies didn't
cry and disease is uncomfortable and that villages are fun
only because you knew the feel of good leather on good
pavement
they cried when they saw mercedes benz were as common
in lagos as volkswagens are in berlin
they shook their heads when they understood there was no
difference between the french and the english and the
        americans
and the afro-americans or the tribe next door or the country
across the border

they were exasperated when they heard sly and the family
    stone
in francophone africa and they finally smiled when little
    boys
who spoke no western tongue said "james brown" with
    reverence
they brought out their cameras and bought out africa's
    drums
when they finally realized they are strangers all over
and love is only and always about the lover not the beloved
they marveled at the beauty of the people and the richness
of the land knowing they could never possess either

they clapped when they took off
for home despite the dead
dream they saw a free future

[29 aug 71]

Poem

(For Anna Hedgeman and Alfreda Duster)

thinning hair
estee laudered
deliberate sentences
chubby hands
glasses resting atop ample softness
dresses too long
beaded down
elbow length gloves   funny hats
ready smiles
        diamond rings
hopeful questions
needing to be needed
my ladies over fifty
who birthed and nursed
my Blackness

[8 jan 72]

Atrocities

in an age of napalmed children
with words like *the enemy is whatever moves*
as an excuse for killing vietnamese infants

at a time when one president one nobel prize winner
one president's brother four to six white students
dozens of Black students and various hippies
would be corralled maimed and killed

in a day where the c.i.a. could hire Black hands to pull
the trigger on malcolm

during a decade that saw eight nurses in chicago
sixteen people at the university of texas along with
the boston stranger do a fantastic death
dance matched only by the murders of john coltrane
sonny liston jimi hendrixs and janis joplin

in a technological structure where featherstone
and che would be old-fashioned bombed

at a moment when agnew could define hard and soft
drugs on the basis of his daughter's involvement
with them

in a nation where eugene robinson could testify
against his own panther recruits and eldridge cleaver

could expel a martyr from that martyr's creation
where the president who at least knows
the law would say manson who at least tried
is guilty

it is only natural that joe frazier
would emerge

[8 mar 71]

Nothing Makes Sense

a bright sun flower yellow tiger
was at my bedroom door teeth bared ready to pounce
when the child cried "the bear is gonna get me!"
and i completely understood cause i had to really
wake up fast to keep that tiger back

nothing is real especially
tones i heard
a rumbling and thought
the world was coming
to an end

and saw my body blown to bits and crushed under
the rubbish that had been the 100th street apartment
complex my guppies struggled for one last breath
and my turtle   head hidden in his shell   never
to fuss again at me for not cleaning him

the blinding light started in the 96th street subway
and quickly swept up to my house melting my flesh
into the cactus plant at my bedside and as my hand blended
into a thorn i wondered what it would be like to never
hold anyone again

what never was cannot be
though it engulfed me and i cried
"what always is   is not the answer!"

they came from all over the world in planes
in boats and dirigibles
on kites and pollen seeds riding bikes
and horses bare back on electric roller skates
and lionel trains all carrying an instrument to play
or blow and bleat and the sound called all the carnivores
from all over the world the aardwolf and the puma playing
the talking drum even the snow leopard with a long thin
hollowed ice flute came from his himalayan retreat
and all the snakes over ten feet long slithered through
the heavy traffic to my house to play a mass
and through the altos and basses and your condescending
attitude aretha started a low moan

the outline of a face on a picture isn't really
a face or an image of a face but the idea of an image
of a dream that once was dreamed by some artist
who never knew how much more real is a dream than reality

so julian bond was elected president and rap brown chief
justice of the supreme court and nixon sold himself
on 42nd street for a package of winstons
(with the down home taste) and our man on the moon said
        alleluia
and we all raised our right fist in the power sign
and the earth was thrown off course and crashed into the sun
but since we never recognize the sun
we went right on to work in our factories

57

and offices and laundry mats and record shops
the next morning and only the children
and a few poets knew
that a change had come

[22 jan 72]

I Laughed When I Wrote It

(Don't You Think It's Funny?)

the f.b.i. came by my house three weeks ago
one white agent one black (or i guess negro would be
more appropriate) with two three-button suits on (one to
    a man)
thin ties—cuffs in the bottoms—belts at their waists
they said in unison:
    ms. giovanni you are getting to be quite important
    people listen to what you have to say
i said nothing
    we would like to have to give a different message
i said: gee are all you guys really shorter than hoover
they said:
    it would be a patriotic gesture if you'd quit saying
    you love rap brown and if you'd maybe give us some
        leads
    on what some of your friends are doing
i said: fuck you
a week later the c.i.a. came by two unisexes one blond afro
one darker one three bulges on each showing lovely bell-
    bottoms and boots
they said in rounds:
    sister why not loosen up and turn on
    fuck the system up from the inside
    we can turn you on to some groovy
    trips and you don't have to worry

59

about money or nothing   take the commune
way and a few drugs it'll be good for you
and the little one
after i finished a long loud stinky fart i said serenely
definitely though with love
    fuck you
yesterday a representative from interpol stopped me in the
    park
tall, neat afro, striped hip huggers bulging only in the right
place
    i really dig you, he said, i want to do something for you
    and you alone
i asked what he would like to do   for me
    need a trip around the world a car bigger apartment
    are you lonely i mean we need to get you comfortable
    cause a lot of people listen to you and you
    need to be comfortable to put forth a positive image
and digging the scene i said listen i would sell
out but i need to make it worth my while you understand
    you just name it and i'll give it to you, he assured me
well, i pondered, i want aretha franklin and her piano
    reduced to fit next to my electric
typewriter on my desk and i'll do anything you want
he lowered his long black eyelashes and smiled a whimsical
    smile
    fuck you, nikki, he said

    [7 jan 72]

On Seeing Black Journal and Watching Nine Negro Leaders "Give Aid and Comfort to the Enemy" to Quote Richard Nixon

it wouldn't have been
so bad if there had
been a white rock group singing
"steal away" from the side lines
(at least that would have made it
honest)

it is not too late/is too/is not/yah yah/so yo mama/is not
"Sir would you keep your remarks
succinct" said straight face
to people who were used to talking hours and never
sucking cint

"come with me—i mean come to me—that is i got rhythm
        —i mean
i can orchestrate and harmonize and ooo wee can i do a
        militant
shuffle"

"well i'm from small plains oklahoma and i want
to know about the sewer problem

just how should black people approach them"
"would whoever answers please
just be brief   we have important calls
from all over the country!"
"i want the integrationists to go on
record   just where do you stand
on sewers?!!!??!*?
          chorus

                    oh jesus was a lovely cat
                    he taught us how to pray
                    and every night we get on our knees
                    and this is what we say:
                              oh i hate the white man
                              i love the white man
                              and it's just a natural fact
                              that one way or other if you stick around
                              he'll get on your back
and what about naomi?
for the answers to these and other important questions
like: do we have any Black leaders
stay tuned to (music please————)

the sets were turned off
the white men stood up   scratched themselves
and said well we're good for another
four hundred years or so

the Black youngsters turned off
their sets got down
on their knees and prayed
                    oh lord please
                    don't take the honkie
                    away

          [13 feb 72]

And Another Thing

i'm leaving at five
she said why
are niggers always
late

a circle he replied is
a sunbeam that saw
itself and fell
in love

niggers would be
late for their own
damned funerals

it's the early bird
he whispered in her
ear that catches the worm
but no one ever said why
the worm gets up

how we gonna get this
country moving when we can't
get together
on such simple shit

sometimes he said brushing
her afro back with his rough hands
you scrub clothes to remove
a spot and sometimes you soak
them first

you not even listening to me

you're not listening to me

they looked at each other
for a moment

and another thing
she began

[18 feb 72]

We

we stood there waiting
    on the corners
    in the bars
    on the stoops
    in the pews
    by the cadillacs
    for buses
    wanting for love
    watching to see if hope would come by
we stood there hearing
    the sound of police sirens
    and fire engines
    the explosions
    and babies crying
    the gas escaping
    and the roaches breeding
    the garbage cans falling
    and the stairways creaking
we listened
    to the books opening
    and hearts shutting
    the hands rubbing
    the bodies sweating

we were seeing the revolution screeeeeeeeeeching
    to a halt
    trying to find a clever way
    to be empty

    [2 feb 70]

My House

i only want to
be there to kiss you
as you want to be kissed
when you need to be kissed
where i want to kiss you
cause it's my house
and i plan to live in it

i really need to hug you
when i want to hug you
as you like to hug me
does this sound like a silly poem

i mean it's my house
and i want to fry pork chops
and bake sweet potatoes
and call them yams
cause i run the kitchen
and i can stand the heat

i spent all winter in
carpet stores gathering
patches so i could make
a quilt
does this really sound
like a silly poem

i mean i want to keep you
warm

and my windows might be dirty
but it's my house
and if i can't see out sometimes
they can't see in either

english isn't a good language
to express emotion through
mostly i imagine because people
try to speak english instead
of trying to speak through it
i don't know maybe it is
a silly poem

i'm saying it's my house
and i'll make fudge and call
it love and touch my lips
to the chocolate warmth
and smile at old men and call
it revolution cause what's real
is really real
and i still like men in tight
pants cause everybody has some

thing to give and more
important need something to take

and this is my house and you make me
happy
so this is your poem

[26 feb 72]